CLUB MUSE MAGAZINE
2010
VOLUME ONE: ISSUES 1 & 2

CLUB MUSE MEDIA

Family Folklore Foundation, Inc.
http://familyfolklorefoundationinc.org

"CLUB MUSE MAGAZINE" is distributed internationally by
Blue Moon Publications.

P.O.B. 662   Crown Point, IN 46308-0662

Family Folklore Foundation, Inc.
Our mission is to offer educational opportunities to
intergenerational community members using
literacy and problem-solving strategies to make the

world a better place.

Our goods are the magazines and documentaries we create from our events. Their sales finance our mission, allowing for a portion to be given back to the community. Our services are designing events based on community interests, and implementing the events.

President-Dr. Meg Grandfield DeMakas, author, illustrator, professor, educational consultant.

Vice-President-Kathleen A. Anton, Registered Nurse, business owner, visiting nurse, artist, humanitarian.

Treasurer-Karen A. Wagner, administrative assistant, volunteer, naturalist, organic gardener.

Secretary-Margaret Johnson, personnel, merchandizing, home engineer, humanitarian.

FOUNDATON EVENTS
January 15, 2010 Lakeshore Focus
National Public Television Show
Dr. Meg G. DeMakas appears on show to discuss the spring project of Family Folklore Foundation, Inc. with Dr. Daniel Lowery, who views the magazine and some documentary clips!

March 19, 2010 "Historical Stories, and Artifacts, and Fossils, Oh, My" Field Trip
The 4th Grade from South Haven Elementary

School in the Portage Township Schools will be experiencing a field trip to the Valparaiso Public Library, the Memorial Opera House, and the Porter County Historical Museum in downtown Valparaiso, Indiana, from 11:00-1:30. VOLUNTEERS ARE WELCOME, as are DONATIONS!!!!

Students will learn about the history of the area while being televised for a documentary called, "Farragut's Folks". The 4th graders will also write articles about the field trip experience for a magazine by the same name.

May 17, 2010
"Night in the Opera House and Museum" Tickets for the event are $1.00 a piece. The price of the magazine is $1.00. You can buy tickets and magazines at the door or in advance. The 'Silver Screen' will be lowered at the Memorial Opera House for a 7:00-8:00 p.m. media blitz of the documentary / magazine issue, "Farragut's Folks". The 4th Grade Choir will sing Indiana favorites. Between 6:00 and 6:45 and 8:15-9:00 p.m. the Porter County Historical Museum tour guides will conduct tours of the museum.

SUMMER EVENT
www.kankakeevalleyhistoricalsociety.org/
August 28, 2010 AUKIKI FESTIVAL AT THE KANKAKEE HISTORICAL SOCIETY!!!
10 am until noon in Kouts, Indiana. (Same day as the Kouts Pig Roast!) Post Trib reporter and

photographer interview and take pictures!
Learners of all ages come learn by experience. Join
the fun with people dressed in historical costumes
of pioneers, Native Americans, and voyageurs. See
an archeological dig! Enjoy the food, music,
games, and other entertainment of life when the
Collier Lodge was inhabited by people of the
past! Participants will videotape the morning and
later write about their impressions for the second
issue of the Club Muse Media Magazine.

SEPTEMBER 25, 2010 REGIONRAMBLER.COM **Crown
Point Hall of Justice 6:30 Presentation of Family Folklore
Foundation, Inc. Seth and Dr. Meg as puppeteers, Mac
Larson reading his article about the buckshot pouch, and a
trailer video about the projects thus far!**

**October 29, 2010 "Ghosts of Kankakee Past" 7:30-9:15
pm. SHARE OUR FIELD EXPERIENCE WITH
COMMUNITY MEMBERS IN THE COMFORT OF
THE ARM CHAIRS OF THE PORTER COUNTY
MEMORIAL OPERA HOUSE!
We will present our magazines and film at Memorial
Opera House.**

**SUMMER EVENT 2011
WILDFLOWER WOODS, GENE STRATTON-PORTER
HISTORICAL SITE
NOBLE CITY, IN**

FARRAGUT'S FOLKS
BY THE SOUTH HAVEN ELEMENTARY 4TH GRADE

CLUB MUSE MEDIA MAGAZINE

ISSUE I, VOLUME I, MAY 2010

familyfolklorefoundationinc.com

'Farragut's Folks', a Club Muse Media magazine issue, presented at 'The Night at the Opera House and Museum' media blitz on May 17, 2010 in collaboration with 'Farragut's Folks' Club Muse Media Documentary at the Memorial Opera House in Valparaiso, Indiana. It is brought to you by Family Folklore Foundation, Incorporated, a nonprofit organization, whose purpose is to educate the community via experiential learning, and magazine & documentary creation.

Sources:
John D. Wolf, "With Captain David Porter or How We Got Our Name Valparaiso and Porter County, Indiana" 2007
A Variety of Encyclopedias, Dictionaries, and Internet Sources

Credits:
Perry Cozza, Janet Smith, Rebecca Swerdon, Teachers, &
Chris Evans, Principal, South Haven Elementary, PTS
Kevin Pazour, Director of the Porter County Historical Society Jail Museum
Brian Schafer, Director of the Memorial Opera House & Expo Center
John Wolf, Author, "With Captain David Porter or How We Got Our Name Valparaiso and Porter County, Indiana"
Daniel Lowery, Star of 'Lakeshore Focus', PTV Channel 56
Willow Cataldo, Larry Clark, and Staff, Porter County Main Library
Robin Witte, Architect, Chester, Inc.
Courtney Carstens and Julie Larson, Purdue University Calumet Students
Jessica Renslow, Film Producer, and Lindsey Myers, Film Editor
Chris Messer, Director of Photography
Photographs and Drawings Compliments of South Haven School Family

Booklet Sponsored by
Valparaiso Rotary Club
Dr. Stephen Grandfield

Printing
American Printing
May 2010

Dr. Meg G. DeMakas, CEO, Family Folklore Foundation, Inc.
For more information contact: megdemakas@familyfolklorefoundationinc.org

'FARRAGUT'S FOLKS'
ARTICLES BY SOUTH HAVEN 4TH GRADE
Based on Historical Field Trip to the Memorial Opera House, the
Porter County Jail Museum, and the Porter County Main Library

Articles by Mr. Perry Cozza's 4th Grade Class
David Porter by Izabella Batey & Emily Luck

David Porter was born in Tennessee February 1, 1780. He became a naval officer and
was the captain of the ESSEX. On the ESSEX, Porter led his crew on a raid into the
Pacific Ocean that help destroyed the British whaling industry. The War of 1812 was
fought between the United States of America and the British Empire. It lasted from 1812
to 1815. It was fought chiefly on the Atlantic Ocean and on the land, coasts, and
waterways of North America. David Porter died in March 3, 1843.

War of 1812 by Alexis Jones & Kayla Brown

The War of 1812 was fought between the United States and Great Britain from June 1812
to the spring of 1815. The peace treaty ending the war was signed in Europe in December
1814. The mainland fighting of the war occurred along the Canadian border, in the
Chesapeake Bay region, and along the Gulf of Mexico. Much action also took place at
sea. The war confirmed American Independence and the British army was successfully
stopped when it attempted to capture the cities of Baltimore and New Orleans.

World War I Helmet by Noah Penrose

The World War I helmet that I saw was bumpy,
smooth, and hard. It is still dirty but cool. It has a strap on it, too. From the top to
bottom, it is twelve centimeters and it's seventy-two centimeters around the head. The
helmet is green and brown and it is still rusty. It is almost one hundred years old.

Old Jail Museum by Kayla Corral, Chris Jett & Cheyanne K.

The building is very interesting. It was built in 1862. Thomas Edison came to Valparaiso in 1880 to talk about electricity. The Old Jail and the former Sheriff's residence were named to the National Register of Historic Places on June 23, 1976. You can walk through the Museum and then go to the jail because they are connected. The museum is the home of many historical treasures of Porter County.

MAMMOTH TUSK
by Frank Griffin, Drew Lopez, & Michael Carlisle

Mammoths lived about 10,000 years ago. They belong to the elephant family. Their tusks are about 13 feet and their bodies were 14 feet wide. Mammoths are prehistoric. Mammoth fossils are found in Europe and in almost every state of the United States. These mammoth bones were found in Porter County, Indiana. Mammoth bodies are found perfect in the ice. Alaskan mountain climbers find them, and Alaskan miners find petrified mammoth bones, too.

Mammoth by Skylar Szparaga

The mammoth's tusk was about 10 feet long. There were several species of mammoth. Some were big and others were not so big. The largest mammoth is Sungar Mammoth, which was 5 meters tall and is heavier than Tyrannosaurus Rex! But the most famous mammoth is the Woolly Mammoth. It was the size of a modern day Asian elephant (around 3 meters tall). Mammoths are the ancestors of the elephants and are mammals. They were on our planet 10,000 years ago.

Museum Arrowheads by Mimi Ramos

You can find arrowheads almost anywhere in our area. They are sharp around the edges! They are very small but rock solid! Some weigh as much as a small book and are very colorful. The one that I saw was tan, yellow, light brown, and pink. I did not know that many arrowheads can be found in local farm fields. The one I saw was shaped like a Christmas tree.

Arrowheads by Tara McGucken & Heather Ellis

Our arrowheads looked like a Christmas tree and a fish. Heather's arrowhead was very smooth and Tara's arrowhead was very hard and bumpy. Tara's length was six centimeters and Heather's was eight centimeters. Our arrowheads were tan and black in color. They are made of sharp stone and could later be attached to a bone. They were attached to the front end of a spear by the early Native Americans and used as a weapon or tool for hunting.

The Saber-Toothed Tiger by Randy Revetta & Angel Orta-Gonzalez

The saber-toothed tiger was a prehistoric animal. The saber-toothed tiger lived about 40 million years ago. The saber-toothed tiger got its name from its teeth because of the saber shape. They were agile and could run very fast for short distances. They could weigh up to 1,000 pounds. Fossils have been found all around the world. Saber-toothed tigers were much bigger than the tigers of today. The cat's teeth were 8 inches long but they could have been longer.

The Memorial Opera House by Amanda Miletich & Cassie Branham

The Opera House is 117 years old and was built by the Civil War Veterans. The Opera House is an old building and has a trap door in it. The stage can hold 34 to 36 actors. The Opera House does plays. For the plays the people wear costumes. President Lincoln got assassinated in a 'loge' or balcony box seat at the Ford's Theater. The Opera House is called the Memorial Opera House. It was built in 1893.

Articles and Article Excerpts from Mrs. Rebecca Swerdon's Students

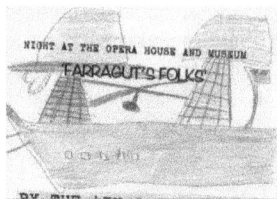

Mr. Wolf's Talk by Zack Gertzen

We went to the library and sat down. Then Mr. Wolf started to talk about Captain Porter and David Glasgow Farragut .He said, "David Farragut was riding the ESSEX in the Battle of Valparaiso, Chili".

David Porter or Captain Porter and Our Field Trip by Jenessa Allen

A ten year old boy joined the United States Navy in 1810 as a commissioned officer and a couple days ago I got to learn about his life. Learning about his life was part of an adventure, our field trip to downtown Valparaiso.   I'll tell you about it. Our first stop was the opera house. That's where they were working on the play 'Beauty and the Beast'. They said they used their imagination to make plays from books. Then we got to see the dressing room and the trap door. Our 2nd stop was the library, where we got to learn about David Porter, David Farragut, his adopted son, and the battle at Valparaiso, Chili. The library has the journal Captain Porter kept about his journey. We got to see Mr. Wolf the author who wrote with Captain David Farragut. Then we went to the Genealogy Room were the 100 year old legal records. After that we ate lunch for 20 minutes, we went to our last stop for the day, the old jail museum. They had cool artifacts I loved the trip! At the end of the day I didn't want to leave because it was fun, educational, and a very good fun experience! On are way back I was thinking about our trip and I hope I go back soon!

James Farragut By Kaitlynn Clasen

We are learning about Captain Porter and also James Farragut. David Farragut's father, James, and Porter's father worked together. When James Farragut died, Captain Porter adopted David Farragut. Porter wanted David to work with him so he got a midshipman's commission. They both went to the Valparaiso, Chili in the U.S.S. Essex, and they were one of the 10 % who survived. They are both brave as lions.

Captain Porter By Ciara Gutierrez

A warship in those days had limited space for its 322 people. Captain Porter's cabin was in the stern of the gun deck. Officers had tiny staterooms on the berth deck, three floors down below was the crew slept here.

'FARRAGUT'S FOLKS'

Captain Porter by Halie Minard
Ten-year-old Midshipman David Glasgow Farragut was Captain Porter's adopted son. Captain Porter had to trust his adopted son, David Farragut, with his jobs on the ship, the Essex.

David Farragut by Cassie Borowicz
In 1810 at age 10, Farragut joined the U.S. Navy as a commissioned officer, a midshipman. During the War of 1812 with the British the ESSEX was a fantastic battleship.

David Farragut by Kamryn Crosby
Farragut's father was a Spaniard adopted American who fought in the Revolutionary War and was friends with David Porter. When his real father died, David Porter adopted him. David Farragut was born on July 5, 1801. David Farragut was 10 years old when David Porter adopted him and joined him in the navy. David Farragut was a very good midshipman. The ESSEX was home to 300 sailors, 10 officers, and 12 midshipmen. The ESSEX was built for speed and had thirty two guns. She was a important to the young navy.

Memorial Opera House by Matt Rebec
In the opera house Brian told us that there was a new play coming out. It is "Beauty and the Beast". If you want to go, a ticket is 20 bucks.

The Memorial Opera House by Samantha Laingren
The Opera House has live plays. It was built in honor of the people who fought in the Civil War. The Opera House is 117 years old. There is a trap door. When we went there, they working on "Beauty and the Beast'.

THE OPERA HOUSE by Sam Carlisle
At the trip we had to see the STUFF in the dressing room. We had to fit in the small room that they get dressed in. Then they have to get set for the Show. They can get on the show with the trapdoor that puts them on the stage. Then they start the show. And they have to move stuff all around the stage. They have to get a upgrade on the old stage because it was so old. It was built in 1885. That a long time ago! .And it is 2010. When they're done with a show the actors write on the brick wall behind the stage. It was So cool!

THE OPERA HOUSE by Kevin Branhan

The opera house is about where people are doing plays. In a few weeks they are playing 'Beauty and the Beast'. In the stage floor there is a trap door so the actor can come up magically.

The Memorial Opera House by: Kayla Hovey

I'm here to tell you about the Memorial Oprah House which is 115 years old. We toured and saw the trap door, dressing rooms, and tried on costumes.

Memorial Opera House by Alison Revetta

I am writing about the Memorial Opera House. When we went they were putting the stage together for a play called: 'Disney's Beauty and The Beast'.

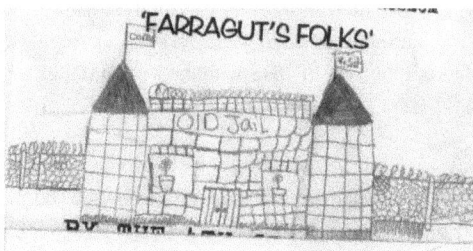

Old Jail Museum by Angel Sanchez

At the museum we saw the old jail that they use to keep prisoners in!!! The prisoners broke out because they used sandstone instead of cement. When the prisoners were out the police found all of them put them in jail and used cement instead of sandstone!!! Right now in the jail museum the bars are cut down and there are exhibits of guns, foxes and all kinds of stuff. It's really neat, you should go to our media blitz on May 17th!!!!! It only costs one dollar for the video show and one dollar for the magazine you can see what we experienced!!!!!!

World War 1 Army Helmet by Nathan Rogers

When I tried on this artifact hat and felt like I was in a battle. I knew that it was old because of the dust.

OLD JAIL by Codey Marlow

I LIKE THE OLD JAIL BECAUSE IT HAD COOL ARTIFACTS. THERE WAS A SECRET TUNNEL THAT THE SHERIFF USED TO CHECK THE CELLS SO NONE OF THE PRISONERS WOULD GET OUT. I WAS STARING AT A CHAIR THAT WAS IN ONE OF THE CELLS. IT HAD A COLLECTION OF BONES ALL OVER IT. IT WAS A MUSEUM EXHIBIT.

The Old Jail by Malina Reber

At the old jail we saw many artifacts. My favorite was the old phonograph. There was a tunnel in the jail too, that I also liked walking through.

The Old Jail Museum by Lexie Cipich

I am writing about The Old Jail Museum. At The Old Jail Museum Kevin talks about arrowheads and other artifacts.

Mammoth and Mastodon by Todd Bangs

The huge elephant-like animals called mammoths and mastodons disappeared from the earth before historic times. The bodies of the mammoths were covered by a furry coat of wool.

The Old Jail Museum by Cindy Lewis

At the old jail museum the Director, Kevin, was showing an old music player and behind him is a very old wheel chair. Downstairs is a lot of Indian stuff.

The Porter County Historical Jail Museum by Drew West

It all started in 1906 when people just got out of control so they made a jail so people could do time and learn their lesson. Some prisoners got out by shaking the bars, but they got put back in the jail. Now the walls are made of cement instead of limestone.

The Old Jail by Conner Berti

At our fieldtrip we saw the   museum. First it was a jail. The prisoners got out because the sand stone walls. The sheriff got them back in there and made the walls out of cement. It is now a museum.

The Old Jail by Niko Janes

Have you ever been to the jail in Valparaiso? It's small, and interesting! the jail is to the sheriff 's house once the people in the jail escaped by shaking the bars and the bars broke. They fixed the bars into limestone. They caught the people and put the back in jail.

Architect at Museum by Kaitlynn Clasen

I liked learning how buildings are unique. We learned how to design a house.

The Articles by Mrs. Janet Smith's 4th Grade Class

Jail House Museum Artifacts
Chris Spencer, Tristan Hargett, Erick Maldonado, & Josh Nicholson

One artifact there was a pre-arrowhead. The reason why it is called a pre- arrowhead is because the Native Americans messed up in making it and couldn't or wouldn't fix it. The way stone weapons were made was by somebody tapping a stone and tapping another stone in certain places. What would happen is, as your tapping the stone with another stone pieces would fall off of the stone your tapping.

The next artifact we are going to talk about is the Frag Grenade. The Frag Grenade was used in World War 1 and World War 2. It was also used in the Korean War and the Vietnam War. In the Grenade is a fuse when you pull the pin in matter of seconds the grenade will explode. The squares in the grenade will pop out when the grenade explodes and the squares will fly around until it hits something.

A saber tooth tiger's skull was one of the artifacts at the museum. This skull was found in Porter County. Saber teeth were about 5 inches long. All of the bones of the tiger were there. If you go to the museum and you want to see the skull, look for the mastodon tusk and look up. This is our article, good-bye.

Jail Museum
by Jordan Chambers, Mickayla Edmaiston, and Austin King

What we saw at the museum is a variety of things from the past owners of the house. What caught our attention was a tree that had the Civil War weapons in it. One of the unique weapons was a missile.

There was Native American things from a past owner. Some of the things were an Indian dress head, a buffalo skin, and many tools.

It was such a fun experience to see the historical sites in Valparaiso.

My Family by Jillian Guined

I don't know a lot about my family. I do know that my papa's dad used to beat him so he ran away. So he took a train to where his sister lived. I think she lived in Tennessee. So he lived with her. He went to school and worked many jobs. Then he met my mama after she graduated high school.

The Opera House
by Jaimie Bailey, Chris Martin, and Melissa Boswell

If you go to the Opera House there are few things to suspect. On one wall they put the names of plays and the years that they showed them in spray paint, but you can't see it from the audience. The reason is because of the set and the curtains. Under the stage there is a trapdoor to lift the actors onto the stage with an elevator. The people who are in the plays go into a basement to dress up and put their make up on. There is also a pit where the orchestra plays their instruments.

The Memorial Opera House by Samantha Marsh and Julianne Lopez

If you ask me, visit the Porter County Opera House. I give it 5 stars, but it's your choice. If you favor classic plays, the Opera House is where you should be! You've got your adrenalin-pumping horror movies, and your classic fairytales. If you're looking for a fun, family movie for some fairytale loving girls, the Opera House is premiering Beauty and the Beast. Down stairs there is the dressing room. In there is where everyone gets dressed up as the person they are in the play. In the next room (which is the makeup room) the people get to look like the person they are in the play. (makeup, wigs, etc.) If you stand in a certain spot downstairs, you will see the trap door elevator system that takes the people that are on stage down stairs and the people that are downstairs up on the stage.

The Jail Museum by Myles Davis, Kale Nelson, Alexis Brown, and Kenny Clasen

When we went to the Jail Museum in Valparaiso we saw artifacts and fossils. Two of the artifacts were a spearhead and a hammer stone . The Native Americans used these things to hunt and to put things in the ground.

Some other artifacts that were at the museum were a petrified cocoanut and a gramophone. The gramophone was created by Thomas Edison in 1888. The cocoanut was found in Hawaii by someone from Porter County.

When we went into a different room we saw a tusk and the tour guide told there was a secret sheriff hallway. The tusk is from a mastodon. There are so many artifacts in the sheriff's hallway that we can't explain them all.

Mr. Cozza's Class at the Library

Mrs. Smith's Class at the Opera House

Mrs. Swerdon's Class at the Museum

COLLIER'S CLUB HOUSE, Baum's Bridge, Kouts Postoffice, Porter Co., Ind.

(Photos by the Kankakee Historical Society)   Collier Lodge 1910

Aukiki Festival 2010
Kankakee Historical Society

"Ghosts of Kankakee Past"
Family Folklore Foundation, Inc.

familyfolklorefoundationinc.org.

MEDIA BLITZ AT OPERA HOUSE

On Friday, October 29th, from 7:30-9:15, the "Ghosts of Kankakee Past" film and second magazine issue of Club Muse Media will be available to the public at the Valparaiso Memorial Opera House. Donations for the event are always appreciated! (Costumes are Optional!)

The Family Folklore Foundation Nonprofit Corporation's mission is to educate the community via experiential learning and multi-media. If you can't make the field trips, you can watch the films and read the magazines in the comfort of a theater armchair!

Sources:
John D. Wolf, "With Captain David Porter or How We Got Our Name Valparaiso and Porter County, Indiana" 2007
Aukiki Day 2010 presented by
Kankakee Historical Society Collier Lodge

Credits:
Almost Fairy Tales Films
Special Thanks to Jessica Renslow, Editor
Lindsey Myers, &
Andrew Renslow, Narration
Chris Messer, Director of Photography
Walmart Community Grants

Printing:
Area Career Center Digital Printing
October 2010

"Ghosts of Kankakee Past" Club Muse Media Magazine Issue #2 October 2010. Copies available at:
familyfolklorefoundationinc.org.
megdemakas@familyfolklorefoundationinc.org.

"Ghosts of Kankakee Past" Media Blitz
By Dr. Meg G. DeMakas,
CEO, Family Folklore Foundation, Inc.

The Family Folklore Foundation, Inc. participants went into a proverbial time machine and landed at the Aukiki River Festival of the Kankakee Historical Society Collier Lodge for our second film, "Ghosts of Kankakee Past". We also interviewed local historian, Dr. John Wolf, about how Porter County and Valparaiso got their names. Our members' reflections form the script of the film, as well as the magazine issue articles. The boys, Mac Larson and Seth Odenthal videotaped this time, wielding tripods cranking out 360 degree camera views. We used music from the Brown musicians, who played pioneer music at the festival. Then the video clips and scripts went to Hollywood for production.

Coming to the Aukiki Festival is reminiscent of Shakespeare's line, "Life is ....but ...a stage". Walking into the forest lined meadow with campfire smoke, cannon sounds, and people from the past milling around is, indeed, a jaunt into the past. Only from such forest primeval would one find Scottish tradesmen, Pottawatomie wigwams, French Voyageurs, and pioneer musicians peaceably meandering at the edge of the Kankakee River. Time travelers of Family Folklore Foundation, Inc. discovered more about life discussing the ways of the Aukiki festival players than in any history book or movie! They discerned more about life in 2010 from artifacts, narratives, and historical reenactments than Googling , Cable, and texting their friends.

COLLIER'S CLUB HOUSE, Baum's Bridge, Kouts Postoffice, Porter Co., Ind.

Julie Larson, and Sister, Mallory Demoff

The Kankakee River is rich in history, dating back to 8000 B.C. We know this because of the artifacts found here in recent years. Part of this history is the Collier Lodge. It was built to house the men in the Hunt Club. Important men from near and far came to hunt duck, including former Presidents, Teddy Roosevelt and Grover Cleveland are known to have hunted here. It was a prime location for this sport.

HISTORY COMES ALIVE!
Potawatomie and the French Voyageurs
By Mrs. Darlene Martinez

The life of the Potawatomie woman was a hard one. To make a shirt, for instance, it took a week! First you have to kill a deer, then skin it, tan the hide, etc. Or if you make a shirt from cloth, you have to weave the cloth at a pace of an inch per two hours. It is easy to see why the Indian women were so glad to see the French Voyageurs arrive with their trading goods! They could trade dried meat for woven clothing!

(Photo of 2004 Dig)
Archaeologist by Seth Odenthal (and Janna)

A man is digging a large, deep square hole under a tent. It looks really fun and fascinating, so I am watching him. His name is Mr. Mark Shurr. He said he teaches anthropology at Notre Dame. He really loves history, just like I do.

He is doing a project for the Kankakee Valley Historical Society at a place called Collier Lodge. Not very many people get to be this close to a real live archaeology dig. Mostly I just read about them in books about people who dig for dinosaurs in the desert, or I see it in a museum. But now I'm actually getting to see a part of it, up close!

Mr. Shurr is looking for some items that Indians and people used a really long time ago. It must be very hard to do so much digging. Some of the ground is dark dirt, some of it is sand, and some of it is light dirt. It is neat to see the grass roots and how far they go down. There is a lot more stuff in dirt than I realized. It's more than just bugs and worms and stuff.

He is digging very carefully with a small shovel. He has the square marked off with lines made out of string. After he digs some dirt out, he is giving it to some people that are helping him. They are putting the dirt on some screens that are attached to a wooden stand. Then they are sifting through the dirt to find tiny pieces of clay, bone, rocks and other things.

When the helpers find things, they are putting them in little plastic bags and labeling them so they remember what it is and where it was found. Mr. Shurr is making a chart to record the items and in what section each one was found.

He is good at explaining things to me. He is so excited about what he is doing here. He seems to be finding a lot of things. I'm glad he's letting me be a part of it. I hope he keeps digging so I can keep watching each year. Maybe some day I can help him!

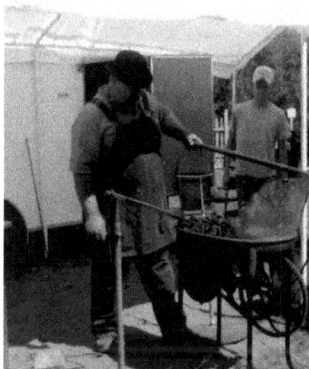

The Buckshot Pouch
By MacKenzie Larson

When Dr. Meg showed me her fossils and artifacts I was amazed. There was a giant sea shell, some really great books, and a trilobite fossil. The one thing she let me carry was a buckshot pouch. Buckshot is something hunters use for ammo. We found an English hunter who knew a lot about guns and ammunition. I showed him the pouch and he said it had a broken spring in the lever. So I took it over to the blacksmith to see if he could fix the lever. He said unfortunately didn't have the tools. That is okay, maybe it is better to leave history the way it is.

Brown Musicians at Aukiki Festival 2010

Mallory and Julie Larson

When we arrived at the entrance to the Aukiki River Festival the sound of tribal beats filled our ears. A lone Indian played his hand carved drum he found in Taos, New Mexico. These were not the only musical tones of the day. We heard familiar tunes from a team singing folks songs while playing various instruments; a dulcimer, spoons, harpsichord and guitar. The music was inviting and fun to sing along too. On our way out there was a banjo player singing a ditty or two. The music put a smile on all of our faces.